WHITNEY

ANIMALS AT THE EDGE

ANIMALS AT THE

EDGE

SAVING THE WORLD'S RAREST CREATURES

Jonathan Baillie & Marilyn Baillie

MAPLE
TREE
PRESS

Maple Tree Press Inc.
51 Front Street East, Suite 200, Toronto, Ontario M5E 1B3
www.mapletreepress.com

Distributed in Canada by Raincoast Books
9050 Shaughnessy Street, Vancouver, British Columbia V6P 6E5

Distributed in the United States by Publishers Group West
1700 Fourth Street, Berkeley, California 94710

Dedication
For my two little explorers, Alexander and Ana – J.B.
For my children and grandchildren, with love – M.B.

Acknowledgments
A warm thank-you to Publisher Sheba Meland, Executive Editor Anne Shone, and Associate Editor Cali Hoffman. An appreciative thank-you to Carly Waterman and the dedicated EDGE scientists and EDGE Fellows, as well as the Synchronicity Foundation. A special thank-you to Claudia Dávila for her creative design work.

Cataloguing in Publication Data
Baillie, Marilyn
    Animals at the EDGE : saving the world's rarest creatures / Marilyn Baillie, Jonathan Baillie.

Includes index.
ISBN 978-1-897349-32-8 (bound).   ISBN 978-1-897349-33-5 (pbk.)

    1. Rare animals—Juvenile literature. 2. Endangered species—Juvenile literature.
3. Wildlife conservation—Juvenile literature. I. Baillie, Jonathan II. Title.

QL83.B36 2008   j591.68   C2008-902041-3

Library of Congress Control Number: 2008925714

Design: Claudia Dávila

We acknowledge the financial support of the Canada Council for the Arts, the Ontario Arts Council, the Government of Canada through the Book Publishing Industry Development Program (BPIDP), and the Government of Ontario through the Ontario Media Development Corporation's Book Initiative for our publishing activities.

ONTARIO ARTS COUNCIL
CONSEIL DES ARTS DE L'ONTARIO

Printed in China

A   B   C   D   E   F

CONTENTS

Meet the World's Rarest and Most Unusual Creatures   6

Forever Gone   8

Saving the World's Rarest Creatures   10

Attenborough's Long-Beaked Echidna   12
In Search of Attenborough's Long-Beaked Echidna   14

Yangtze River Dolphin   16

Hispaniolan Solenodon   18

Long-Eared Jerboa   20
In Search of the Long-Eared Jerboa   22

Bumblebee Bat   24

Pygmy Hippopotamus   26

Slender Loris   28

Hirola Antelope   30

Golden-Rumped Elephant-Shrew   32

Aye-Aye   34

Wild Bactrian Camel   36
In Search of the Wild Bactrian Camel   38

On the EDGE and on the Map   40

Glossary   42
Index   44
Photo Credits   45
About the EDGE Project   46

MEET THE WORLD'S RAREST AND MOST UNUSUAL CREATURES

Within these pages you will meet amazing animals you have never heard of before. Each animal is the last of its kind alive on this Earth. Some have no close relatives, others have very few. These creatures are so rare, not much is even known about them.

You will find magical creatures such as the long-eared jerboa, a kangaroo-like animal no bigger than a mouse, and a strange relative of the elephant that looks like a shrew. You will encounter the shy pygmy hippopotamus, and the tiniest mammal on Earth, the bumblebee bat. And then there is the secretive solenodon, a nighttime

Pygmy hippopotamus (above)

Bumblebee bat (right)

Long-eared jerboa

mammal that has a venomous bite like a snake. Not only are these animals different from all other creatures, they are also extremely rare and may disappear forever from our planet if they are not protected.

You will also meet the scientists who are on the move around the world working towards a safe future for each of these creatures. Join the excitement of following the scientists as they study each animal up close.

Golden-rumped elephant-shrew

BACK FROM THE EDGE

The animals you're about to encounter are all part of the Zoological Society of London's EDGE (Evolutionarily Distinct and Globally Endangered) project. The project was started to highlight these unique creatures so they do not silently disappear from our world forever. It focuses on species that are unusual and endangered, where little or no attention has been given to save them. To learn even more about the project, see page 46.

Forever Gone

EXTINCTION IN THE PAST

Wouldn't it be great to see a dinosaur clomp down your street? A little scary, too! Of course, dinosaurs became extinct long before humans were on this Earth.

Preserved animal bones, or fossils, tell us stories about gigantic mammals that lived here after dinosaurs ruled the Earth. Perhaps you have heard of the wooly mammoth, or the fierce, saber-toothed tiger? How about the awkward giant ground sloth? And there was teratornis, the huge vulture with a wingspan wider than your outstretched arms. These animals all became extinct many years ago.

Now, what about today? Would it surprise you to find out that many animals are disappearing right before our eyes?

A saber-toothed tiger bares its knifelike teeth.

From dinosaur bones in museums, like this theropod's skeleton, we can imagine what awesome creatures they were. This dinosaur lived 112 million years ago.

The now extinct wooly mammoth, a relative of the elephant that existed during the Ice Age.

EXTINCTION IN THE PRESENT

What weird creature had features of a wolf, a tiger, and a kangaroo? This odd combination adds up to a thylacine. Just 75 years ago, the thylacine roamed the open forests of Tasmania. Some called this animal the Tasmanian tiger because of its stripes. You might have thought it looked like a wolf. But what a strange wolf it would be! The thylacine mother carried her pups in her pouch. When four pups were crowded in together, the pouch would hang almost to the ground.

Thylacines were one-of-a-kind animals. Now they are all gone. What happened? Settlers hunted the thylacine to protect their sheep. The government even paid people to kill the thylacine. In time, there were fewer and fewer of these animals and then, sadly, there were none.

Saving the World's Rarest Creatures

Scientists are keen detectives. Some study the habits of endangered animals where the animals live. This fieldwork can take scientists to faraway, even dangerous places. Scientists study the reasons for the animals' decline. Some causes can be mysterious, others hidden.

From this fieldwork, the scientist makes an Action Plan identifying what needs to be done to protect the species. Finally it is time to put the Action Plan to work to save the animals. Conservation continues with the help of local people who see how special their natural treasures are and want to protect their animals, too.

OUT IN THE FIELD

Have you ever thought about what it is like to be a scientist studying an animal in the field? If you want to learn about an animal's habits, where its home is, what it eats, or how many young it has, you follow that animal. You climb mountains, stomp through swamps, or brave the desert sun. Sometimes you sit silently for hours waiting, watching, and listening, and then waiting some more.

When you pack your backpack for a field study, you must carry everything you will need. Don't forget your clothes, food and water, a good tent, your binoculars, your camera, and a map. Depending on the animal you are studying, you might also need some research tools. Have you packed pitfall traps (see left), camera traps (see lower right) or a bat detector (top right)? Now, can you carry your pack?

MEET THE SCIENTISTS

As you discover the world's strangest and most threatened animals, you will meet the dedicated scientists working to save them. Their studies take them to distant places to make discoveries. Go along on the adventure with them.

ATTENBOROUGH'S LONG-BEAKED ECHIDNA

Is Attenborough's long-beaked echidna alive or extinct? Dr. Jonathan Baillie has gone into the field to try to solve the mystery.

Long-beaked echidnas are rare mammals called monotremes. The mother echidna lays an egg, and carries it in a pouch. Only five species of mammals lay eggs. All other mammals give birth to live young.

Home to an Attenborough's long-beaked echidna is a distant peak in the Cyclops Mountains in faraway Papua. Not much is known about these secretive creatures. At night, the echidna probably follows its snout to hunt for earthworms and insect larvae. It doesn't need teeth. Its tongue is layered with spikes that hook and pull its prey into its mouth.

No photos of a living Attenborough's echidna exist. The echidna shown is a close relative.

Don't try to pick up an echidna. They are covered in sharp spines that stand up when they are frightened. After the little one hatches, it cuddles inside its mother's pouch and suckles her milk. Soon it grows its own spiky spines. Now it is time to move out.

Local tribespeople believe that the echidna has unusual powers to keep peace within the tribe.

MEET THE SCIENTIST

Dr. Jonathan Baillie

I have wanted to work with animals for as long as I can remember. My mother used to find my tadpoles swimming in the kitchen sink, and stray animals in my bedroom. I started working in Central Africa, where I lived in the jungle, studying western lowland gorillas. Like gorillas, echidnas are endangered. They are different from all other species. I want to make sure people know how special these creatures are.

Jonathan's Notes

Key questions for me:

- Is the Attenborough's echidna extinct?

- If the Attenborough's echidna still exists, where in the mountains are they the most common?

- What is causing them to die out?

- If there are still some, what can be done to save them?

IN SEARCH OF ATTENBOROUGH'S

Field Notes from the
Cyclops Mountains, Papua
Scientist: Dr. Jonathan Baillie

When we arrived in the mountains, I spoke with local villagers to find out if there was a word for the echidna in the local language. I wanted to know if any of the villagers had seen one recently. I learned that they call the echidna "payangko," and a local hunter had caught one as recently as two years ago. This gave me hope that echidnas were still living in the mountains.

No one could tell me if echidnas were found high in the hills, as villagers never venture into the top peaks of the mysterious mountain range. We asked permission from the local tribe to climb the steep mountain, and went on our way.

We spent many days high up in the steamy mountain forests, looking for signs of echidnas.

LONG-BEAKED ECHIDNA

It was extremely hot as we trekked through the forests, and blood-sucking leeches were continually trying to sneak into our boots.

After searching for a long time, we finally came across a few sites where we could see the echidnas had been feeding. When an echidna eats, it puts its long beak, and sometimes even the top of its head, in the ground. This leaves a distinct print in the earth known as a nose-poke. We were ecstatic to find that the Attenborough's echidna is alive and well in the mountains!

After the field study, I know the echidna still lives in the Cyclops Mountains—from the base to the cloud forest at the top. I know where in the mountains it is most common, and that hunting is the greatest threat to the echidna's future survival.

WHAT'S NEXT?

I am working with local students to develop an educational program letting the villagers know how special the echidna is, and that it is only found in their mountains. Scientists are working with the villagers to monitor the echidna so we can learn more about its behavior.

YANGTZE RIVER DOLPHIN

DID YOU KNOW?

The baiji is an incredible LONG DISTANCE SWIMMER. It can swim hundreds of miles up or down the vast Yangtze River. It often swims up smaller streams to breed.

In the distance, the dolphins would surface from the deep Yangtze River. The Chinese people tell stories to each other about these graceful water creatures. Could they be princesses dancing through the ripples? Or are they goddesses appearing from the waves? These shy Yangtze River dolphins, or baiji, are cherished in China as national treasures.

Today, there is a huge mystery about them. Are there any Yangtze River dolphins still living in the river?

A recent search failed to find even one. Scientists are hopeful that a few are hiding in the vast and murky river. They are the only living representatives left from an entire family of mammals.

The Yangtze River is one of the busiest waterways in the world. Large cities with millions of people crowd along the river shores. A huge dam is being built that will affect the river creatures. With pollution, boats, and over-fishing, the dolphins' life is almost impossible.

The baiji has tiny eyes. Like other river dolphins, it has little need for good vision in the muddy waters it inhabits.

MEET THE SCIENTIST

Dr. Sam Turvey

DID YOU KNOW?

Hundreds of years ago, Chinese fishermen hunted the baiji for its **SPECIAL POWERS**. They believed that the dolphin's meat could cure a person possessed by evil spirits.

As a child, I spent happy summers full of discovery at a farm in Finland. What could be more exciting than feeding calves, gathering eggs from hens, and spotting freshwater seals and moose in the wild? While in China working with fossils, I became drawn to the Yangtze River dolphin. These baiji were in great danger of dying out but not much was being done about it. Trying to save the baiji is a passionate struggle for me. In such a short time, the baiji has probably now become extinct. I continue to hope that some will be found in the Yangtze River.

Sam's Notes

- Keep asking local fishermen about any recent baiji sightings.

- With my electronic device called a hydrophone, listen for baiji calls underwater.

- If we find any dolphins here, study whether we can move them to a safer part of the river system.

HISPANIOLAN SOLENODON

Who has seen a solenodon? Almost nobody! These rare, squirrel-sized creatures with extra-long noses live quietly on one island in the world. This Hispaniolan solenodon comes from Haiti and the Dominican Republic, on the island of Hispaniola in the Caribbean.

Although the solenodon is small, it has large, strong claws on its feet. It easily digs into the earth for spiders and insects to eat, or it quickly burrows a hole to hide in. The solenodon comes out only at

DID YOU KNOW?

The solenodon's relatives branched off from all other mammals during the time of **DINOSAURS**.

MEET THE SCIENTIST

Osé Pauléus

I have lived all my life in Haiti and I care very much about my island. Haiti was once called the "Jewel of the Caribbean" because of our natural riches, both plant and animal. Many species have disappeared from the past. That is why I feel it is so important to teach people to be proud of what we have and to work together to conserve what is left. I want to make sure that our Haitian wildlife, such as the solenodon, is still here for my children and grandchildren to enjoy.

Osé's Notes

- <u>Done</u>: A survey to find out if solenodons are alive or extinct; more than expected were found here.

- <u>To Do</u>: Study solenodons.

- Attach a small electronic tracking device to some to find out where they go.

- Find the solenodons' homes and study the threats to their life there.

- Make conservation plans.

DID YOU KNOW?

The word solenodon means GROOVED TOOTH.

night. That makes it even harder to spot. But if you should find a solenodon, watch out for its venomous bite. Its front teeth have grooves that carry the venom. The solenodon can't run fast. One chomp and its unusual venom weapon stops its prey.

Much of the solenodon's forest home has been chopped away, and outside animals, brought to the island, hunt it. There is still so much to discover about the mysterious solenodon. Scientists are hard at work to try to solve some of these mysteries.

LONG-EARED JERBOA

Underground burrows provide cool shade during the day. When the sun goes down, the jerboa comes out to hunt for food.

What has a mouse-sized body, legs that jump like a kangaroo's, and ears the size of half its body? This strange creature is the long-eared jerboa. It lives in the harsh, dry desert of Mongolia and China.

The jerboa probably digs itself underground burrows to hide out in during the sizzling desert days. Then the cool nights bring it out to hunt for food. Its special feet are perfect for leaping across the desert. Under each foot is a tuft of stiff hairs that support the jerboa as it takes off and lands on loose sand. Up and away it jumps again and again.

The long-eared jerboa is a mystery. Scientists know very little about this fascinating desert creature. Why are there fewer and fewer of them in the desert? What are its everyday habits? Is there plenty of food for it to find? Is there enough water for it to drink? Searching for answers is how scientists can help save the jerboa.

What advantage is it to have such large ears? Are bigger ears better for hearing insect sounds while hunting at night? Or do extra large ears act as a cooling system? This would give more body surface, allowing body heat to escape in a hot climate.

MEET THE SCIENTIST

Uuganbadrakh Oyunkhishig

DID YOU KNOW?

Some species of jerboa can **JUMP** 1 metre (3 ft.) high and 3 to 6 metres (10–20 ft.) in length. Why don't you try to jump that high and that far, too?

Uuganbadrakh's Notes

- Right now: Estimate numbers of long-eared jerboas by catching them in pitfall traps. When the jerboas slide into a small cone-shaped trap, I count them and gently release them unharmed.

- Search for the jerboa's preferred home areas and study what dangers or threats there are there.

- From this research, suggest a conservation plan.

I grew up in northern Mongolia where my parents taught school. My father was my teacher. He was very much against hunting and taught me to love and appreciate our wildlife. I enjoyed studying biology and was at the top of my class at school. I was lucky to be awarded a scholarship to continue to study biology. My dream is to become one of Mongolia's best scientists. This is my first experience running a field project in the Gobi Desert and I am very excited to be the first scientist to really discover the way the long-eared jerboa behaves and lives its family life in the desert.

IN SEARCH OF THE

Field Notes from the
Little Gobi Desert, Mongolia

Scientists: Uuganbadrakh Oyunkhishig
and Jonathan Baillie

We drove south from Ulan Bator, Mongolia's capital city, for two days until we were just north of the Chinese border. The desert is extremely barren and in some places looks like the moon. In parts of the desert there are no roads and we got lost trying to find our research camp. We climbed up to a high point and Uuganbadrakh spotted the ger (or yurt) in the distance. A ger is where Mongolian herders live.

When we got to the ger, we visited an old woman who had lived in the desert for 96 years. She said there were once many animals in the area but now there are fewer because of hunting and lack of rain.

After chatting with the local herders we headed out to the study site to set up pitfall traps. The traps don't hurt the animals at all, and they can be safely released afterwards.

We used corn, wheat, dried fruit, and smoked fish for bait. The sand and gravel was very hard and it was difficult to dig out the holes to place the metal cone traps in the ground. We hoped a few long-eared jerboas might slide into our traps.

LONG-EARED JERBOA

The rare long-eared jerboa hops out in the cool desert night.

We stayed awake in the ger until three in the morning and then drove in the night by motorbike out to where we had placed the traps. We peered into the first trap and found a Gobi jerboa and in the second trap a Siberian jerboa.

In the third trap we found what we were looking for! It was a beautiful long-eared jerboa. After measuring and weighing it we placed it on the sand and watched it rapidly hop over to a small hill and quickly burrow into the sand. We then continued to check the traps and there were a total of six long-eared jerboas that night.

WHAT'S NEXT?

Uuganbadrakh has continued to try and trap long-eared jerboas in different habitats. He has discovered they prefer sand and gravel sites with small bushes. Uuganbadrakh is now trying to find out what is causing them to decline.

BUMBLEBEE BAT

Tiny and perfect, the bumblebee bat is probably the smallest mammal in the world. People are so enchanted with these tiny bats, they travel all the way to Thailand to see them. They sometimes smuggle them home, killing such fragile animals. These small creatures have no close relatives. They are from a unique family of bats that is very rare and very endangered.

Bumblebee bats dangle upside-down from ceilings in limestone caves in Western Thailand and Myanmar. They like to gather in groups but always find their own little spot to cling to. As soon as the sun sinks or starts to rise, they fly out together to find something to eat. They snatch insects passing by or swoop in on spiders and beetles. Since they are hunting in the dark, they use sound waves to find their prey. This is called echolocation.

Also known as the Kitti's hog-nosed bat, this tiny bat is the size of a bumblebee, just a bump in your cupped hand.

People are
AFRAID OF BATS,
but why? Out of about
1,116 species of bats only
three species drink blood.

There is still so much to learn about the family life and habits of these intriguing flying mammals. Perhaps they can only live in their limestone caves. If the caves are disturbed, will the bats leave and never find another home?

By studying them, scientists hope to soon find out the answers to these questions. We do know they need our conservation help.

MEET THE SCIENTIST

Dr. Kate Jones

I am fascinated with bats! As well as being the only mammals that can fly, they have other remarkable features. The secret sounds bats make to locate and hunt insects flying by is sophisticated and mysterious. You and I cannot hear a thing from their echolocation calls but I can listen to their private chatter at night with my bat detector. This helps me study the complex hunting and feeding habits of bats, and discover where their roosts are. As I spend more time following and studying the bumblebee bat, I can suggest ways to make forest areas safer for these tiny creatures, as well as for other bats that live there.

Kate's Notes

To Do:

- Find any other areas where the bumblebee bats live. Only two places are known so far.

- Use my bat detector to count the number of bats and find out how far they feed from their caves.

- Propose a conservation plan to protect the bats in their home area.

PYGMY HIPPOPOTAMUS

Pygmy hippos spend their days lolling in swamps or resting in rivers. By late afternoon, they head out one by one to feed on plants, grasses, leaves, and fruit. When darkness falls, they follow familiar paths that tunnel through thick vegetation. It is all in a night's work to eat enough green food to fill their large hippo bodies.

The pygmy hippopotamus looks somewhat like its larger cousin, the common hippopotamus. The smaller pygmy hippo has a more rounded head and separated toes instead of webbed feet. Both hippos share a very strange relative. From recent genetic studies a surprise link has been made: hippos are related to whales.

Pygmy hippos live scattered in shrinking numbers in western Africa. The largest group lives in Liberia in Sapo National Park. Some captive breeding programs do exist. Nevertheless, fewer and fewer pygmy hippos are spotted in the wild.

Luckily there are no leopards lurking about. Only this animal would dare attack a hefty hippo.

Dr. Ben Collen

I have always loved wildlife and grew up in England surrounded by it. When I first went to work in Africa, the vast plains brimming with lions, cheetahs, zebras, and birdlife was irresistible to me. My conservation fieldwork focused on endangered animals such as wild dogs, cheetahs, and leopards. Now my research on pygmy hippos takes me to Africa's western rainforests. I use camera traps, special cameras attached to trees, to catch never-before filmed studies of pygmy hippo behavior. Many secrets are unfolding, which help me understand what forest areas need to be protected.

Ben's Notes

Done:

- Study photos from camera traps (I now have the very first photos of a pygmy hippo in the wild in Liberia).

To Do:

- Find out if hippos are raiding the villagers' crops. Hippos are being blamed and killed.

- Help villagers to protect their crops and involve villagers in protecting the pygmy hippos.

DID YOU KNOW?

The pygmy hippopotamus knows how to keep dry underwater. It secretes oils through its pores that are thought to keep its skin WATERPROOF. The thick oil can be pinkish in color and is called "blood-sweat."

SLENDER LORIS

Two gigantic eyes stare down at you out of the black night. The slender loris is taking everything in. Silently, it picks its way along a branch. With its amazing night eyes and keen sense of smell, it is sure to find its food in the dark. The loris is searching for insects but is content to eat leaves, fruit, birds' eggs, and even small lizards.

Nobody knows how many of these furry creatures with the large questioning eyes remain today. Their home is on the island of Sri Lanka, in the rainforests. Although protected by law, slender lorises are sometimes hunted for meat, or perhaps for their mythical, magical powers. As their forest homes are cleared for rubber, cinnamon, tea, and palm oil plantations, slender lorises are left looking for food and shelter.

If the slender loris is so busy all night searching for food, what does it do all day? You'll find it curled up with its friends in the hollow of a tree. There it sleeps the day away.

Carly Waterman

The baby slender loris (see page 48) is just as unusual looking as its mother. There is a proverb in Sri Lanka that says only a mother could love such a **BIZARRE LOOKING CREATURE.**

Great apes, especially orangutans, caught my imagination when I was studying primate animal behavior at university. As I observed orangutans in the wild, I became more involved with the conservation of these peaceful creatures swaying in the branches. As local people started to realize how rare and amazing their neighborhood orangutans were, they too became protective of their intriguing animals. Smaller, unfamiliar primates such as the slender loris also need our protection and attention. That is where my focus is today. I am working with local scientists to do everything we can to help protect these unusual and endangered animals.

Carly's Notes

<u>To Do:</u>

- Work with local scientists to find out loris numbers and loris home areas.

- Get approval to plant trees to join forest areas where lorises move about hunting for food.

- Study local attitudes and myths about the slender loris.

HiROLA ANTELOPE

Sadly, only a few hirola antelope herds roam the East African plains today.

Suddenly, the hirolas take flight. All you hear are their hoofs pounding the ground like beating drums. On long legs, they stream across the grassland in search of a safer place to graze. Not any grass will do. The best are the tasty sprouts just beginning to poke through. As the antelopes bend their heads to eat again, they listen and stay alert. Who knows what might be lurking right next to them? Lions, cheetahs, and hyenas are looking for breakfast, too. The day is just beginning near the coast of Kenya in Africa.

The male leader of the herd is the strongest. He protects his family group of females and young calves. He fights for their territory so there will be enough of the shorter grasses for his family to eat. If drought comes again, the herd will have to keep on the move to find enough grass to live on. Drought means little food or water for all the animals. Many cannot survive.

These beautiful antelopes with their stately horns are the only ones left from a large related antelope group.

Dr. Richard Kock

Today, the hirola is Africa's **MOST THREATENED** antelope. When your parents were young, about 14,000 of these antelopes dotted the grasslands of East Africa. Now there are thought to be fewer than a thousand left.

My brother and I left zigzag paths as we biked through wild bush to our one-room bush school. Our farm in Zimbabwe, Africa, was far away from any other kids. We had a radio but no television, so the two of us made our own fun roaming freely through the forest, ready for any adventure the bush held for us. When I became a wildlife vet and treated captive wild animals, I understood why many of these wild creatures could not survive away from their natural homes. My work as a wildlife vet, initiating animal health programs and conservation, has taken me to many countries and unknown corners of the world. While working in East Africa, I became intrigued with the graceful hirolas and I continue to be committed to their conservation.

Richard's Notes

Action Plan:

- Work with herders to monitor and protect the hirolas, as they do with their own sheep and goats.

- Work with local scientists to study the hirolas and their habits.

- Study the possibility of ecotourism.

GOLDEN-RUMPED ELEPHANT-SHREW

Is the golden-rumped elephant-shrew an elephant or a shrew? It is not an elephant but it is distantly related to elephants. It is not a shrew but it is small like a shrew. And, yes, it does have a golden patch of fur on its rump.

You would have to travel to the coast of Kenya in Africa to find golden-rumped elephant-shrews. They spend the day sifting through leaves on the forest floor. Their long trunk is like a vacuum, poking around to uncover earthworms, beetles, and termites. Then, the elephant-shrew digs out its meal with its two front feet.

Sometimes, all this activity catches the attention of a certain bird. The red-capped robin-chat follows the elephant-shrew through the forest, eating any tidbits left behind.

Bed for the elephant-shrew is a nest made of dry leaves on the forest floor. To be safe, it sleeps in a different nest each night. Forest cobra and black mamba snakes silently slither on the ground, and hawks are on the lookout from above. But much more dangerous for the elephant-shrews is the loss of their forest home. As their forests are fast disappearing, so are these intriguing forest creatures.

Does the elephant-shrew's long nose remind you of a mini elephant's trunk?

MEET THE SCIENTIST

Dr. Nick Isaac

I grew up in the Dorset countryside in England, where I often saw wild animals in the garden and surrounding farmland. I can still remember the excitement of sighting deer, foxes, and water voles. Under a full moon in the summer, we would see hedgehogs congregate on our lawn. Like many biologists, I was really switched on to the wonders of animal life and the complexities of the natural world through Attenborough's nature programs. These things were quite important because biology was never my strongest subject at school. I took a gamble and changed from physical to natural science at university, and I've never really looked back since.

DID YOU KNOW?

Golden-rumped elephant-shrews MATE FOR LIFE. Together, they defend their home area. She chases intruding females away and he chases any males away.

Nick's Notes

To Do:

- Estimate how many elephant-shrews live here by using my mist nets. The nets are so thin the elephant-shrews get caught but don't get hurt. Then I can count them and let them go.

- Find out if elephant-shrews live in other forests near here.

- Research whether elephant-shrews could adjust to a new home area.

AYE-AYE

Aye-ayes rest in their treetop nests during the day, and come out and roam at night.

The aye-aye is one of the strangest-looking animals on Earth. Huge leathery ears flare sideways from its small pointed face. Glowing orange-yellow eyes shine out at you. And thick, wiry fur pokes up from its body. Aye-ayes live in forest areas in Madagascar, an island off the south-east coast of Africa.

Why is the aye-aye thought of as the woodpecker of Madagascar? Aye-ayes are primates and mammals, with amazing long fingers. The aye-aye tap, tap, taps its extra long middle finger against the bark of a tree, like a woodpecker does with its beak.

It cocks its large ears forward and listens for grubs burrowing beneath. There they are! The aye-aye rips away the bark with its teeth and scoops out a delicious grub with its middle finger. Aye-ayes also feed on fruit, fungi, nuts, nectar, and seeds.

In some areas, when an aye-aye is spotted, it is often killed upon sight. Local people believe they are an evil omen. In other areas, farming and development are taking away the aye-aye's forest home. Although captive breeding centers have bred some of these fascinating little creatures, their numbers are dwindling in the wild.

People used to think aye-ayes were related to rats or rodents. Not so. Aye-ayes are **PRIMATES**, and are the largest primates that feed at night.

MEET THE SCIENTIST

Helen Meredith

I first saw an aye-aye when I was eight. There it was, staring through the gloom in the shadows. I could make out the huge ears, furry body, and long delicate fingers of one of Madagascar's strangest and most misunderstood inhabitants. I was at the Jersey Zoo in England. It was Gerald Durrell's zoo, and he's the one who inspired me to become a conservationist. Through his zoo, books, and films, he taught me that no creature is ugly—that every living thing has a fascinating story. One of his last books was *The Aye-Aye and I*, a story about trying to save the aye-aye from extinction. The aye-ayes I'd seen as a child were there to help save their species, and that idea had a profound effect on me.

Helen's Notes

Action Plan:

- Work with Malagasy scientists to study the aye-aye and its habits.

- Study protected forests where the aye-aye is usually found and focus conservation there.

- Think of the best ways to change attitudes about the aye-aye being an evil omen.

WILD BACTRIAN CAMEL

Wild camels usually spend the night sleeping in open spaces, and forage for food during the day.

The wild Bactrian camel lives where most other animals could never survive. The dry, hostile Gobi Desert in Mongolia and China is its home. How is the wild camel so amazingly equipped for its harsh life? It can munch on thorns and dried-up plants, and even drink salty water if the desert is bare. Its two humps store extra fat, food for its body when there is not a thing to eat or drink for several days.

When sand whips against the camel in a fierce desert storm, the camel closes its nostrils to keep the sand out. A double row of long eyelashes and hair inside its ears also stops the driving sand

MEET THE SCIENTIST

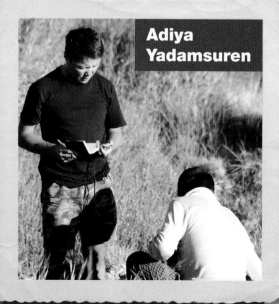

Adiya Yadamsuren

I was born in Western Mongolia and grew up with domestic camels. Camels are an important part of Mongolian culture. They provide transportation and milk for us, and fur for felt. While I was studying biology, I became fascinated with the endangered wild camels and I have worked with different desert expeditions studying these shy, rugged animals. I have come to know their favorite water holes, and followed their tracks for long distances in the Great Gobi Desert. I want to make sure that these hardy animals, which have roamed the Mongolian desert for hundreds of thousand of years, still have a home in the future.

from getting inside. Its sturdy feet keep the camel balanced through the shifting sands and its shaggy coat shields its skin.

The wild Bactrian camel is smaller than its domestic relative. There remain only two areas in the world where large herds of wild camels live today. They are all in China and Mongolia. The Wild Camel Protection Foundation has created a captive breeding center for wild camels. When the young camels are strong enough, they are helped to go back into the desert.

Adiya's Notes

Right Now: I am testing the water quality of the desert water holes the camels use.

- Still searching for wild camels to estimate numbers, see where their habitat is, and where they are having their young.

- Talking with local herders to identify the main threats to wild camels: climate change, illegal mining, or hybridization?

The camel's thick, shaggy fur protects it during the harsh winters, and is shed rapidly in the spring.

IN SEARCH OF THE WILD

Field Notes from the Great Gobi Desert, Special Protected Area, Mongolia
Scientists: Adiya Yadamsuren and Jonathan Baillie

For many parts of our drive, it was not a sand desert, as most people imagine. It was endless, flat planes of baking black pebbles. When the vehicle had to stop due to over-heating, it felt like we were slowly being barbequed.

We started our search for the wild Bactrian camel in the Little Gobi Desert. It took three days to drive from there to the Great Gobi Special Protected Area. At the beginning of the journey we followed dirt roads, and saw domestic camel herders. But soon the roads ended and we had to follow old, dried-out riverbeds. We had to stay in the riverbeds because if we drove on the soft sand, the vehicle would get stuck. We were far away from any town or village.

In this strange, endless landscape, we were lost for some time. But with the GPS (global positioning system), we were able to finally find the Great Gobi Special Protected Area. As we drove through the barren park we saw wild ass, black tailed gazelle, and argali (mountain sheep). Finally, we came across some wild camel footprints, and then an area where the wild camels had been resting. We got out of the vehicle and crawled up a small hill. We peered over. There before us was a large group of 21 wild camels!

They looked quite different from the domestic camels. They were more tan in color, with smaller humps, and flatter-looking heads. They seemed to notice us, but did not seem afraid. After counting them, we were very pleased to see two two-year-olds and two babies in the group—proof they were successfully breeding.

BACTRIAN CAMEL

The wild camels live in such a harsh landscape and are so rare that very few people have ever seen one.

We drove on for 40 km (25 miles) to what was thought to be one of the few permanent water holes, only to find that it was completely dry. We drove another 40 km (25 miles) to the next water hole. It was also completely dry. This means that the camels would have nothing to drink and would have to walk for many days without water. We searched and searched but still no water. Finally, the rain started to fall in torrents, bringing much-needed moisture to the land and animals.

WHAT'S NEXT?

Adiya's task is to continue looking for the rest of the water holes. And this winter he will be conducting interviews with the local camel herders to gather more information about this amazing desert creature.

On the EDGE
and on the Map

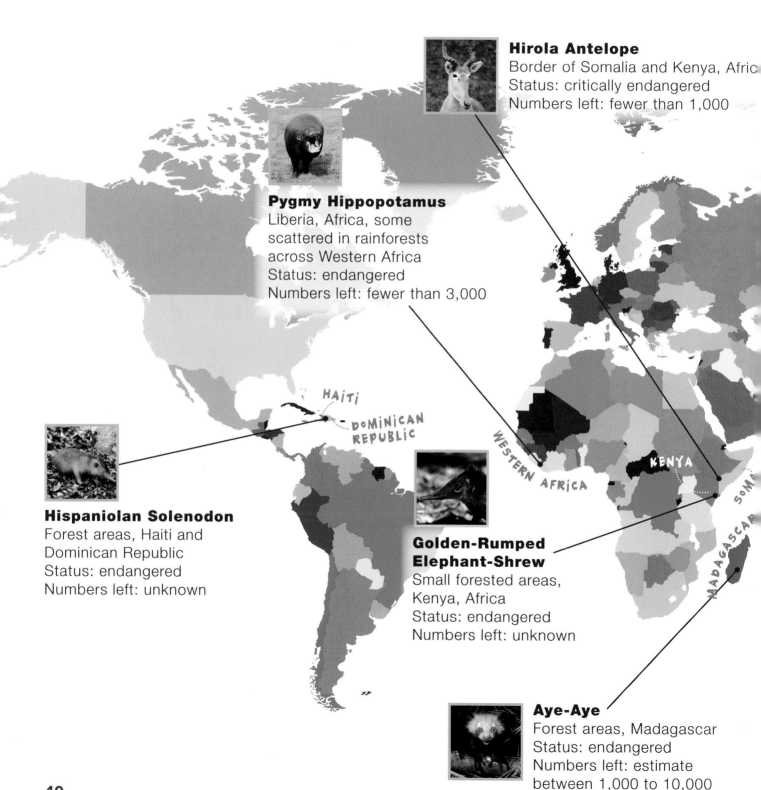

Hirola Antelope
Border of Somalia and Kenya, Afric
Status: critically endangered
Numbers left: fewer than 1,000

Pygmy Hippopotamus
Liberia, Africa, some
scattered in rainforests
across Western Africa
Status: endangered
Numbers left: fewer than 3,000

HAITI
DOMINICAN
REPUBLIC

WESTERN AFRICA

KENYA

SOMA

MADAGASCAR

Hispaniolan Solenodon
Forest areas, Haiti and
Dominican Republic
Status: endangered
Numbers left: unknown

**Golden-Rumped
Elephant-Shrew**
Small forested areas,
Kenya, Africa
Status: endangered
Numbers left: unknown

Aye-Aye
Forest areas, Madagascar
Status: endangered
Numbers left: estimate
between 1,000 to 10,000

Find the faraway places where the EDGE animals live. You will discover their worlds on islands, in jungles, in rivers, and hidden in distant deserts.

If you tell your friends about these weird and wonderful creatures, you are helping to put unknown endangered animals on the map.

Wild Bactrian Camel
Gobi Desert, Mongolia and China
Status: critically endangered
Numbers left: fewer than 1,000

Long-Eared Jerboa
Gobi Desert, Mongolia
and China
Status: endangered
Numbers left: unknown

Yangtze River Dolphin
Yangtze River, China
Status: critically endangered,
perhaps extinct
Numbers left: perhaps none

**Attenborough's
Long-Beaked Echidna**
Cyclops Mountains, Papua
Status: critically endangered,
very rare
Numbers left: unknown

Slender Loris
Southern rainforests,
Sri Lanka
Status: endangered
Numbers left: unknown

Bumblebee Bat
Western Thailand and Myanmar
Status: endangered
Numbers left: unknown in Myanmar,
perhaps 2,000 in Thailand

MONGOLIA

CHINA

MYANMAR

THAILAND

SRI LANKA

PAPUA NEW GUINEA

GLOSSARY

Adapt
To change to fit a new situation.

Bat detector
Small electronic device that picks up the frequency of bat calls.

Biologist
A scientist who studies forms of life.

Camera trap
A special weatherproof camera that reacts to movement. It can be attached to a tree to photograph animals that pass in front of it.

Captive breeding
The breeding of animals in protected enclosures or zoos.

Conservation
Preservation, especially of the natural world or environment.

Decline
To become fewer.

Domestic
A tamed animal, not wild.

Echolocation
Locating or finding an object by reflected sound. Bats send out soundwaves that bounce back off objects to help them find their prey in the dark.

Ecotourism
Tourism intended to support conservation of the natural environment.

Endangered animal
A species so rare, it may die out or become extinct.

Environment
Surroundings affecting all creatures living there.

Extinct animal
Animal that has died out.

Forage
Go searching for food.

Fragile
Delicate, not strong.

Genetics
The study of how traits are passed from one generation to the next.

Ger
Traditional transportable home of Mongolian nomadic people. The tent-like structure is also called a yurt.

Global positioning system (GPS)
A satellite-based navigation system.

Habitat
Natural home of an animal or organism.

Habitat destruction
Destroying or ruining an animal's natural home.

Hostile
Unfriendly, harsh.

Hybridization
Two different species that breed and create offspring.

Hydrophone
Submersible sound sensor device that "hears" or picks up underwater sounds.

Impact
To have a strong effect on.

Increase
To become more through the production of young.

Introduced animals
Animals brought from somewhere else.

Mammal
Warm-blooded animal with a backbone; feeds its young milk.

Mist net
Lightweight mesh net used by scientists. A small animal walks or flies into it and gets caught but not hurt.

Monotreme
Rare kind of mammal that lays eggs.

Myth
A story explaining popular ideas or natural happenings.

Pitfall traps
Container (sometimes cone-shaped) dug into the ground with the top part level to the surface so an animal slides in and cannot get out. Scientists use the traps so they can study animals and then release them back into the wild unharmed.

Prey
Animal hunted or killed by another for food.

Radio-tracking
A small radio transmitter attached to an animal allows scientists to follow, locate, and study the animal's movements.

Primate
Highly developed order of animals: includes humans, apes, and monkeys.

Roosts
Place where bats or birds settle for rest or sleep.

Species
Similar individuals that are able to interbreed or have young.

Survive
Continue to live.

Unique
One of a kind.

Wildlife sanctuary
Place of refuge for animals.

INDEX

A
Action Plan 10
Africa 13, 26, 27, 30, 31, 32, 34, 40
Attenborough's long-beaked echidna 12, 13,
    14, 15, 41, 47
Australia 9
Aye-aye 34, 35, 40, 46

B
Baillie, Dr. Jonathan 13, 14, 15, 22, 38
Bumblebee bat (Kitti's hog-nosed bat) 6, 24,
    25, 41

C
Caribbean 18, 19
China 16, 17, 20, 22, 36, 37, 41
Collen, Dr. Ben 27
Cyclops Mountains 12, 13, 14, 15, 41

D
dinosaurs 8, 13, 18

E
Earth 6, 8
EDGE project 7, 40, 41, 46–47
England 27, 33, 35
expeditions 14, 15, 22, 23, 38-39
extinction 8, 9, 13

F
fieldwork 10
fossils 8

G
giant ground sloth 8
glossary 42, 43
Gobi Desert 21, 22, 36, 38, 41
Golden-rumped elephant-shrew 6, 7, 32,
    33, 40

H
Haiti 18, 19, 40
Hirola antelope 30, 31, 40
Hispaniolan solenodon 6, 18, 19, 40

I
Isaac, Dr. Nick 33

J
Jones, Dr. Kate 25

K
Kenya 30, 32, 40
Kock, Dr. Richard 31

L
leeches 15
Long-eared jerboa 6, 7, 20, 21, 22, 23, 41

M
Madagascar 34, 35, 40
map 40–41
Meredith, Helen 35
Mongolia 20, 21, 22, 36, 37, 38, 41
Myanmar 24, 41

O
Oyunkhishig, Uuganbadrakh 21, 23, 47

P
Papua 12, 14, 41
Pauléus, Osé 19
Pygmy hippopotamus 6, 26, 27, 40

S
saber-toothed tiger 8
Sapo National Park 26
scientists 7, 10, 11, 15, 16, 17, 19, 20, 21,
    25, 27, 28, 31, 33, 35, 36, 37
Slender loris 28, 29, 41, 47, 48
Sri Lanka 28, 29, 41

T
Tasmania 9
Tasmanian tiger 9
teratornis 8
Thailand 24, 41
thylacine 9
Turvey, Dr. Sam 16

W
Waterman, Carly 29
Wild Bactrian Camel 36, 37, 38, 39, 41
wooly mammoth 8, 9

Y
Yadamsuren, Adiya 36, 37, 38, 39
Yangtze River 16, 17, 41
Yangtze River dolphin (baiji) 16, 17, 41, 46

Z
Zoological Society of London 7, 46–47

PHOTO CREDITS

EDGE

About the EDGE Project

The Zoological Society of London's EDGE of Existence program is a global conservation initiative—the only one of its kind. It focuses specifically on threatened species that represent a significant amount of unique evolutionary history. Using a scientific framework to identify the world's most Evolutionarily Distinct and Globally Endangered (EDGE) species, the program highlights and protects some of the most uncommon and wonderful species on the planet.

EDGE species have few close relatives on the tree of life. They are often extremely unusual in the way they look, live, and behave, as well as in their genetic make-up. These species represent a unique and irreplaceable part of the world's natural heritage, yet an alarming proportion are sliding silently towards extinction unnoticed. The aim of the EDGE program is to put these species on the map and promote conservation action to secure their future.

Visit www.edgeofexistence.org to follow the ongoing work of the EDGE group.

The Zoological Society of London (ZSL) is a charity devoted to the worldwide conservation of animals and their habitats.

zsl.org